This 'Oil' Painting was by the Artist Jessie Larman.
Representing a Vision that a Christian Lady wanted painted.

It is Vision of Jacobs Ladder going up to Heaven.
*

You will find the story in
Genesis: Chapter 28 verses 10 - 15

For God so loved the world, that He gave His only begotten Son, that whosoever believeth in Him should not perish but have everlasting life.

John: Chapter 3 verse 16.

Jesus is Lord

May God our Heavenly Father Bless You Today

. . . .

Whether you are a new or mature Christian,
I pray that God will bless you
as you use,
read and pray from this book.

. . .

Written & Illustrated by: J.M.R. Larman.
©
Carnarvon Art Studio
P.O. Box. 149
Carnarvon.
Western .Australia 6701.
www.carnarvonartstudio.com

Blogs:
www.praybibletruths.wordpress.com
www.basketsofgodsflowers.com

e Book: Flowers for the Altar

e-mail: j.larman@wn.com.au

National Library of Australia Cataloguing-in-Publication entry
Creator: Larman, Jessie author, illustrator.
Title: True stories of God / Jessie Mabel Rosina Larman, author +illustrator.
ISBN: 9780987207524 (hardback)
ISBN: 9780987207500 (paperback)
ISBN: 9780987207517 (ebook)
Subjects: Jesus Christ--Divinity--Ancedotes.
God (Christianity)--Biblical teaching--Ancedotes.
God (Christianity)--Attributes--Ancedotes.
Holy Spirit--Biblical teaching--Ancedotes.
Dewey Number: 232.8

Acknowledgements:
✳ ✳ ✳

Special thanks and blessings for helping to edit this book go to My Christian Friend - Mrs. Judy Shaw.

Also Thank you and God Bless to all who have helped this Book come to Fruition.

Scripture quotations taken from the Holy Bible,
New International Version.
Copyright © 1973, 1978, 1984
by International Bible Society.
Plus Old King James version of the Bible.

Some quotes graphic etc., taken from my 'Book of Prayers'

Jesus is Lord

John Chapter: 15 verse 5

*I am the Vine; you are the Branches.
If a man remains in me and I in him,
he will bear much fruit,
apart from me you can do nothing.*

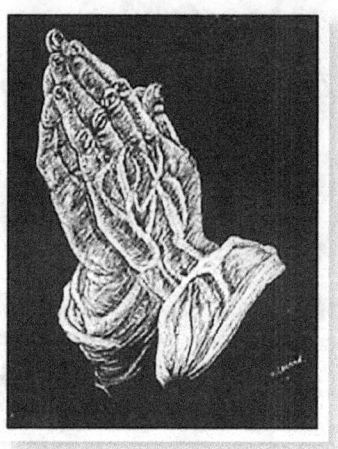

Prayer is Powerful

Never Underestimate the Power of Prayer.

Jesus Is Lord

Lord of all the Earth
Lord of all Creation.

He Is My Lord
Is He Your Lord?

He Reigns on High in Heaven
Angels Bow Down Before Him
& Praise Him Forever More

He is The Lord
He is God's Only Son
And He Is Alive.

True Stories

My Journey with Jesus began.

On a normal Sunday morning my sister and I went to Church. I was five years old at the time and during our Sunday School time sitting on the floor in front of the congregation the Minister (Priest) asked us children to put our hand up if we would like to invite Jesus into our life.

The Priest did explain what it meant so that us younger ones could understand - so, yes I put my hand up - then yes - Jesus came into my life.

I was so excited that when we were home that evening sitting around the fire in the parlour (My Mother, Nanna and Nanna's friend who we called our Auntie Elsie) were getting us children ready for bed, I was just bursting to tell them. So sitting on my Aunt's knee, I told them what had happened during the morning Sunday School. - They seemed to be quite shocked at what I had done.

But Aunt Elsie said it would be for the best as I do believe that she did know more about God. She said now I would have to be a good girl all the time and not tell lies and be nice to people especially to my Mother and Sister.

Well as far as I know I had never told lies. Maybe I was not so good with my sister, as she usually wanted to pick a fight with me. One time hitting me over the head with an iron rod while we were playing in the back garden!

Not long after I had invited Jesus in, the devil stepped in and tried to take my life. I was ill for a long time with pneumonia in hospital, then went home to recover, which took quite a long time. We lived with my Grandmother who we called Nanna i.e. my Mother's Mother. My father was in the Army at the time - this was during the Second World War.

I won't go into details here regarding the illness as that is covered in my Book 'Jessie's Story'.

I do remember getting better, jumping up and down, singing Sunday School songs etc., on the big double bed that I shared each night with Nanna, so that she could look after me during the night. I also used to sing some of the everyday songs of the time.

At night we went to bed with candles and/or a tilly lamp, plus a chamber pot which was put under the bed (no electricity then). Also we had a wash jug and basin in the bedroom - no bathroom. Showers were unheard of then so we had to have a strip down wash standing in the bedroom.

Nanna used to wash me as I lay on the bed until of course I was better. Then I had to learn to wash my body standing there in the room. We did have a tin bath that used to be brought into the Parlour so when I was able to go down stairs I could share in the bath once a week.

One morning I thought I heard Nanna calling so, I got out of bed and went to ask her what she wanted me for - she was in the kitchen come laundry at the time and said 'No I did not call you go back to bed'. So back I went. Then I thought I heard her call 'Jessie, Jessie' so down the stairs I went a second time 'No' she said, she did not call me.

Then back to bed I went and after few minutes - again I heard my name being called.

There was only Nanna in the house that morning apart from myself, so back down I went and she said "You naughty girl I have not been calling you - that's three time you have come down and you should be in bed. You are not well enough to be up yet".

Then she said "Wait, if you are sure you heard your name being called it may have been God calling you. You better go back and say "Here I am God is it you calling me" just like Samuel did in the Bible" - so that is what I did.

I was happy that it was God who was calling me but I do not remember that He said anything at that time. Remember I was still only around five years old.

This happened of course after I had invited Jesus into my life.

Jesus is Lord

In - 1Samuel: chapter 3 verses 1-21
you can read about God
calling Samuel.

My Nanna was a wise and caring lady.

We lived with her until my Father was demobbed from the Army when the Second World War ended in 1945. I was eight years old in the year that the war ended.

For a quite a while my parents had to wait until a house was found for them to live in with us children, which now numbered three (yes by then I had a new baby sister).

Sometimes it's good to look back at the good things that happened in our lives. Inviting Jesus into my life as a five year old child, I had no idea that God would use me in my later years writing books to let others know that Jesus is Alive.

Amen.

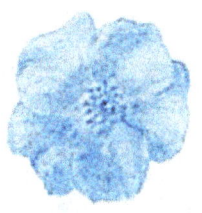

*I sought The Lord and He heard me
and delivered me from all my fears.
Psalm: 34 verse 4*

Jesus is Lord

Light of God

The year 1949 as a 12yr. old.

One evening Nov/Dec during the Winter in England I was taken into the Colchester Hospital Emergency and I was (diagnosed with Bronchial Pneumonia) while I lay on a hospital trolley in the Out Patients Dept.,

With my parents around the bed, plus the Doctor and nurses, I heard the Doctor say 'she may not last till the morning'. Then they all left me there while they must have gone to the Doctors consulting room.

Laying there as a twelve year old girl I prayed to God - our Heavenly Father, asking if I could stay on this earth a bit longer to help my Mother with the children because she found it hard to cope with a big family.

The room seemed to fill with light while I lay there praying and I believed God had answered my Prayers. It was awesome being in the Presence of God, there was no fear just a lovely peace.

I was in the hospital three months as the infection went on to become Double Pneumonia and Pleurisy.

Eventually I was allowed home. Over the coming years God allowed me to help with the children. We became a family of seven children, whom I loved and cared for, hoping one day to have a family of my own.

Over all the years I was quite ill, therefore missed quite a lot of schooling but always had my brothers and sisters around me.

As an eighteen year old I had a lobectomy - (that meant a third of my left lung was cut off). The Operation took place in the Royal Brompton Hospital in London, U.K.

This took a long time of recovery but all the time I knew that Jesus was with me.

Yes God has answered many of my Prayers. Allowing me to be married and have three children that no one thought would ever be possible.   Amen.

At this present time I have Grandchildren and even Great Grand children.

It is good to look back and remember about being in the presence of God our Heavenly Father, while laying on that Hospital trolley in the Outpatients Dept. Amen.

Lunch Time Deliverance:

My young Granddaughter was eating her lunch while I had started washing some dishes in the kitchen sink. I had my back to her and heard her say in an angry sort of voice - 'I am not eating this'. I replied that she should hurry up and eat it. But no, the odd defiant voice came back saying 'no way that she would eat it'.

She never used to talk this way so I turned around to look at her and saw a dreadful grimace on her face. I turned back to wash the dishes and quickly prayed in the Spirit and commanded that thing that was not of God to leave her.

Well suddenly there was a whooshing sort of sound . As I turned to face her that thing left. She put her hands up to her face and said 'It's gone, it's gone, what's gone Nanna, it's gone'

I said it's alright now you can eat your lunch, it was a silly thing that's gone. She was too young to understand that Jesus had allowed a deliverance of an evil spirit to leave her.

Yes, she ate and enjoyed her lunch.

I praise The Lord for His Holy Spirit that commanded that thing to go off of my Granddaughter and out of the house.

I must say it was a bit daunting but I am glad we could do it and of course Jesus gave us protection and God's peace as I felt a bit shaken by the experience, as it involved my lovely young Granddaughter who of course knew nothing regarding the event.

With God all things are possible, we must try not to condone evil things but get rid of them as soon as we can. Amen.

The Lord Worked Quickly:

At our Mother's and children's group, The Lord worked quickly when a small child fell and cut his lip.

His Mother was holding him crying with his lip cut and bleeding from the fall.

She was saying 'help what can I do, can we pray'?

Then as I touched his lip with one finger saying "Jesus help - please heal' the blood just stopped and the child stopped crying.

The Mother was amazed and so was I.

God works in mysterious ways His wonders to perform.

Our children are precious -

In the Bible:

Matthew Chapter 19 verse 14:

Jesus said, "Let the little children come to me and do not hinder them, for the kingdom of heaven belongs to such as these."

Jesus is Lord

What's in a name?

While visiting whilst on holiday I was shown an eighteen month old child who was laying flat on the floor on his Stomach. He had never sat up or crawled and could do none of the normal baby things. - he was destined to stay in that condition for his life time on this earth.

At their son's birth that they had named him spelling his fathers name backwards. Thinking it was funny and laughing saying that he may be backward because his name was spelt backwards.

The very young parents didn't realize that was a curse that needed to be broken. When I was told about his name I was quite shocked to hear they had done such a cruel thing to a precious baby.

Then - having prayed for him, Praise God the next day he was able to lift himself onto his hands and knees into a crawling position for the first time in his young life.

Yes he grew up to walk and run but sad to say is still needing a lot of care as he cannot look after himself.

Maybe one day a cure will hopefully be found for mentally challenged children and adults.

Names are very special as they do affect the child. Also when the child grows to become an adult the name is important to that person.

I believe children can often grow into the likeness of the name that has been chosen for them .

Here is a version of The Lords Prayer.

Most versions differ from each other but the meaning is always the same, this is the way that I particularly like to pray this Prayer.

**From St. Luke: Chapter 11 verse 2
in your Holy Bible.**

...

Our Father who art in Heaven,
Hallowed be your Name.
Your Kingdom come.
Your Will be Done.
On Earth as it is in Heaven
Give us today our daily bread.
And Forgive us our Trespasses, as
We Forgive those who sin against us.
Lead us not into Temptation
But Deliver us from evil.
For Yours is the Kingdom,
The Power and The Glory,
For Ever and Ever - Amen.

...

The Lords Prayer is very special - it covers everything we need to pray for.

Jesus is Lord

Cruise Ship Story.

We were in this large Cruise Ship my husband and I - nothing on it related to a luxury Cruise - but that is not the thing I wanted to talk about today.

Most days I would take my Bible and knitting after our Buffet Breakfast, then find a quiet spot to do my Bible Reading. One morning an older lady came to sit and ask me if I was a Christian or what religion was I, because she recognized that it was a Bible I was reading.

So, yes I told her I was a Christian and after talking for a while she asked if I would pray for her young Grandson who had been diagnosed with cancer and was very ill. I did tell her that maybe she should pray for him but she said she couldn't as she was not sure if God would hear her prayers. Then I said 'Yes of course I will pray for him'. Feeling happy about that, off she went to look for her husband who was wandering around the ship.

A few days later they found my husband and I one evening. Then Phil (the lady who had approached me regards praying) asked if they could join us with a drink in the large bar area of the Ballroom where we were sitting. There was a stage with a live show going on that we were watching at the time when they found us sitting there.

Apparently they had been able to phone home and was told their Grandson was a lot better, so they wanted to thank me for the prayers I had prayed for him.

Then she looked at me and suddenly said "I want what you have". I asked her "What do you mean" and she said "You know" So I said "No, I have no idea what you mean". So we repeated all this again, then she came out with the words "I want what you have in there" touching me in the middle of my chest she said "I want Jesus in me"

Well what a surprise, especially sitting in the noisy area where people were having a drink with their friends while watching a live performance on the stage.

So I suggested we go down to her cabin, there I could lead her in the 'Sinners Prayer' to invite Jesus into her life.

We left our husbands in the ballroom/theatre with their drinks, talking to each other during an interval in the show.
Then in Phil and Bert's cabin we sat down and I asked Phil why she had decided to have Jesus permanently in her life.

"Well" she said most of her family were Christians and she was not sure how to be one, she asked me to explain how. I said that people need to repent of the wrong things they had done in their life and really mean they are sorry and ask Jesus to forgive their sins and come into their heart - then they are born again into the Kingdom of God.

Here is an example of the Sinners Prayer;

Dear Jesus I know I am a sinner I repent of my sins, I do believe that you died on the Cross even for me. Please forgive me and come into my heart to take charge of my life. Thank you that you are now Lord of my life.
I also acknowledge God as my Heavenly Father
and accept your Holy Spirit....
Amen

Of course there different ways to pray the Sinners Prayer but
this is what it is all about to become a Christian.

If you pray the Sinners Prayer and really mean it you are immediately accepted by Jesus.
You are Born Again in the Spirit and belong to the Kingdom of God, Our Heavenly Father.
You need to tell a Christian that you have taken this step.
To speak out is an act of faith and confirms that you have now become a Christian.

Then to begin reading the Bible -
St. John: Chapter 3 verse 16.
Is a good place to start if you decide to take this step.
It says:-
(For God so loved the world that he gave his one and only Son, that whoever believes in him shall not perish but have eternal life.)

May God Bless You with His Love.

*

Back to Phil in the Cabin -

I said to her if she would like to I could lead her in the Sinners Prayer and that she could repeat it with me - if she really did mean that she wanted Jesus in her life.

Now this lady was over eighty years old and I had never ministered to someone this age on my own - in a cabin on a Cruise Ship in the middle of the ocean!

Phil decided to sit comfortably on the small settee and I sat on a chair facing her holding her hands as we began to pray. She repeated after me the prayer to invite Jesus in, then I let go of her hands - laid my hands on her and asked for a special infilling of the Holy Spirit as she had asked me to.

Then all was quiet while I sat back down and waited for her to say something, then the tears started to fall, just running down her face. When I asked if she was alright she just nodded and sat there with a look of absolute peace on her face.

Eventually after what seemed ages, she said that she felt all brand new, that all her troubles had gone away and a big weight had gone from her.

Phil believed that Jesus was with her and insisted that she was not crying. I explained that all the tears were washing her clean from the sins that had been in her life. The whole cabin throughout this time had been filled with a wonderful peace.

So after all that, we went back up to join our husbands who were still watching the show. Phil's face was beaming and they wondered what we had been doing? Phil told Bert she would tell him later.!

Well a few days after this Phil found me on the ship in the same place as before with Pat my husband and said "Bert wants the same". "What do you mean?" I asked. - She said "You know what I mean". Well once again I didn't have a clue what she was talking about - eventually she said "Bert wants Jesus".

What a lovely surprise for a man in his eighties to ask his wife to ask me to do the same for him as I had for Phil. I told her that she could lead Bert in the Prayer like I did for her now that she was a Christian but of course she was not confident at that time to do it.

Also she told me that since she had asked for Prayer for her young Grandchild he was beginning to recover from the cancer even quicker - they had been keeping in contact on the phone from the ship like I had already mentioned.

I had told Phil that as she was now a Christian, Jesus would hear her prayers. She had told Bert this, so he wanted to make sure of the same, that Jesus would hear his prayers.

The other thing that was very important to them both was to know that they would be in Heaven when their earthly bodies died. Because they were both over eighty years old.

So how did we minister then to Bert?

We decided to take Bert down to their cabin and pray for him there, similar to the prayers we prayed for Phil. We sat him on a chair, not on the settee, so that I could ask Phil to stand with me as we placed our hands on his shoulders to pray the sinners prayer with him.

Jesus is Lord

Well he found it hard to hear what we were saying - so it took a while to repeat everything for him but we did it! Nothing dramatic happened but he was sure that he had invited Jesus into his life and repented of his sins. He seemed quite happy about this so we went back up to join Pat who was in the ballroom watching the live show with other friends that we had made on the cruise ship.

A few days later we disembarked, so Pat helped Phil and Bert with their luggage. As Pat walked along the pavement helping Phil, Bert came beside me and said these words:

"You didn't think I was dinkum did you?"

Well what could I say apart from the fact that I was not sure that he had heard alright. He assured me he had heard and touching the centre of his chest as we walked along he said "He is in here and has been hearing my prayers". Bert was very positive about that and so pleased that he had become a Christian even in his eighties.

He had been going to Church with his family for many years but had never thought to ask Jesus to be Lord of his life. Bert and Phil went back to their home in Adelaide and we back to our home in Perth, Western Australia.

A few weeks (maybe a few months) later we received a letter from Phil thanking us for the prayers and saying that their grandson was well.

Praise The Lord that He sees us wherever we are, even on a Cruise Ship in the middle of the Ocean and allows His Holy Spirit to work through us to help bring people into Salvation.   **Amen.**

We cannot hide from God our Heavenly Father.
That can be a great comfort to us knowing that
The Holy spirit of Jesus
is always with us.

Healing of Back

After living in Australia for fifteen years I had travelled back to England to see my family, staying at that time with my Mother. From my Mother's house we could visit most of my brothers, sisters and their families. One particular day we decided to visit my younger sister.

When we arrived her husband opened the front door and informed us that my sister was in bed and that it was not a good time to visit. He was sorry he had been unable to get in touch with us to leave our visit until another day, to save us making a wasted journey.

While telling us this he invited us into the house saying that my sister Jasmine had put her back out suddenly early in the morning and now was confined to bed. Apparently the last time this had happened she could hardly move for about six weeks.

As I was on holiday from Australia and had not seen my sister for 15years I said I was sure she wouldn't mind if we saw her in bed. Having said that - Archie went up stairs to their bedroom to ask if it was alright to visit, then made her presentable for us to see her.

We were allowed up and had our lovely reunion in the bedroom.

While I was giving her a gentle hug I asked in a whisper if she would like me to pray for her back and she said "Yes but not with every one in the room".
Archie had brought their young baby up who he had put on the bed, plus a couple of other children were there, also, my Mother as was the next door neighbour who was visiting.

I silently prayed to ask God if He really would like me to pray for healing of my sister's back could He please get everyone to leave the room.

After a while Jasmine and I asked Mum if she could help Archie make a cup of tea and take the children down stairs, while I would keep Jasmine company till it was ready. Then surprise, surprise everyone went out of the room including the neighbour saying she would talk to Mum while Archie made the tea.

As soon as they had gone out and shut the door - the room was filled with the peace of The Lord. I thanked the Holy Spirit for this and asked Jasmine if she would still like me to pray - having said 'Yes' I asked her permission to put my hand under her to lay it on her back. As she could not move to sit up.

This I did and prayed to The Lord Jesus for healing - I asked her if she believed this could happen and she said 'Yes' and was hopeful that her back would be healed. After the prayer I asked - did she feel any thing? She said "Yes", apparently she had felt a lovely heat on her back. Then just as we finished praying and talking the door opened and in they came with a tray of afternoon tea!

That was all a God Appointment.!

Before we left Jasmine still could not move because of the pain but was glad we prayed and would wait and see what God would do.

Next Morning:

Back at my Mother's house, the next morning I phoned my brother-in-law Archie to ask how my sister was. One of the children answered the phone, so I said "Could I speak to your Dad please I want to ask him how your Mummy is?" He replied "I'll go and fetch her, she is doing the washing".

Jasmine came to the phone with a cheerful voice saying "Hello".
So I said "What are you doing, shouldn't you be resting in bed"?

To which she replied: "No! because you prayed for my back and God healed it during the night, so I am fine now"

During the phone call we both Praised and thanked The Lord Jesus for what He had done.

Jasmine was so relieved that she didn't have to spend about six weeks in bed as she had on a previous occasion.

Jesus is Lord

Praise The Lord God that He allowed Jesus to heal her - what a witness to the family! Amen.

✱✱✱

This really is Good News for Today.

TO BE A CHRISTIAN

Dear Jesus I know I am a sinner I repent of my sins,
please forgive me and come in to my heart to take charge of
my life.
Thank you.
You are now Lord of my life,
I also acknowledge God as Father and accept your
Holy Spirit…....Amen.
…
If you pray the above Prayer and really mean it
you are immediately accepted by Jesus.
You are Born Again (in your spirit) and belong to the
Kingdom of God.
You need to tell a Christian that you have taken this step,
to speak out is an action of faith and confirms
that you have now become a Christian.

You need to begin reading the Bible.
St. John: Chapter 3 verse 3. Says:
Jesus declared, "I tell you the truth,
no-one can see the Kingdom of God
unless he is Born Again."
*

In St. John chapter 14 v 6. Jesus said:
I am the way the truth and the life,
no-one come's to the Father except by me.
…

(May God Bless You With His Love.)

Story of Pat:

Patrick Larman was my Husband. In February 2007 we had been married for 49yrs. We were married 1st. February 1958 when we were both 21yrs old. Pat being six months older than myself.

After not being well for a few years with a blood disorder he was diagnosed with Acute Myeloid Leukemia in July 2006. Pat was not a Christian and took the diagnosis very hard. He had allowed me to go to Church all our married life but although he was brought up in the Roman Catholic faith, (at one time he was an altar boy) he walked away from his faith during his teenage years.

I had asked him to invite Jesus into his life and become a Christian hoping he would do this and pray himself for help with the illness. But he was very aggressive saying it was a load of rubbish and he would not do so.

When he got very ill I nursed him at home - he refused to go into care - so I was able with The Lord Jesus help - to look after him (we needn't go into details about that here).

The main reason to write this is to say that one night when he was in bed and having the oxygen attached, he was holding on to me saying he wanted not to be here. After a while sitting on the edge of the bed I said I must stand up, I can't sit like this all night. - He was propped up on the pillows with the oxygen still there to help him breath. I stood up and said "Why don't you give Jesus a go" (because he wouldn't let me pray for him)!

Well the next minute he sat bolt upright - put his arms straight out and shouted "Alright Jesus you can come in", then he collapsed back onto the pillows.

I stood there stunned, a bit shaken at the shouting because he had not been able to hardly talk for quite some time.

It was marvellous to be able to Praise The Lord that after all those years Pat had at last invited Jesus into his life.

Two days later The Lord took him home to Heaven.

Praise The Lord that Pat asked Jesus to come into his life.

Amen.

Pen & Ink Drawing of Rose Buds

Romans: 5 Verse 8
"While we were yet sinners,
Christ died for us."

Psalm 100 verse 3

Know that The LORD is God.
It is He who made us and we are His people,
the Sheep of His Pasture.

1 John Chapter 3 verse 1

*See what love
The Father has lavished on us,
that we should be called
children of God!*

Jesus is Lord

Love is the Greatest Thing:

This must be a True Story because it says so in the Bible.

1 Corinthians Chapter 13:

Verse I

If I speak in human or angelic tongues but do not have Love,
I am only a resounding gong or a clanging cymbal.

Verses: 4-6

Love is patient, love is kind, it does not envy, it does not boast, it is not proud, it does not dishonor others, it is not self-seeking, it is not easily angered, it keeps no record of wrongs.
Love does not delight in evil but rejoices with the truth.
It always protects, always perseveres.

Verse: 8

Love Never Fails………

Healing as he went:

After Church one Sunday morning we had finished Morning Tea and people were leaving to go home. However one husband and wife stayed to say goodbye to me as they were going to travel further South that day.

Then the wife asked me if I would lay hands on her husband and pray for healing of Emphysema, because he was very ill with it.

So, yes of course I did. We were hoping that The Lord Jesus would instantly heal him. But that didn't happen! They felt very blessed and happy regarding having the prayer time. Being able to share what was wrong with his health, they left to continue their journey.

When they arrived down South they were able to phone me - the lady spoke to me being very excited saying that on the way out of Carnarvon, The Lord healed her husband's lungs as they were driving along.

They were utterly amazed, feeling the presence of the Holy Spirit with them in the car. After that the man had really good health for many more years, they kept in touch by letter a few times after this happened.

Praise The Lord.
Amen.

We can give Glory to God that things happen in His perfect timing.

This is what I call an Olde Worlde Version

23rd. Psalm.

*The Lord is my Shepherd I shall not want
He maketh me to lie down in green pastures;
He leadeth me beside the still waters.
He restoreth my soul;
He leadeth me in the paths of righteousness
for His name's sake.
Yea, though I walk through
the valley of the shadow of death,
I will fear no evil;
for though art with me;
thy rod and thy staff they comfort me.
Thou preparest a table before me
in the presence of mine enemies:
thou anointest my head with oil,
my cup runneth over.
Surely goodness and mercy shall follow me
all the days of my life
and I will dwell in the house*
of the LORD for ever.

*The above is taken from the
Authorized King James Version
of
The Holy Bible*

Jesus is Lord

The Computer

One day a lady knocked on my front door, I had met her about once a year at a Christmas Party but other than that I knew very little about her.

So she knocked on my door that day in the morning and asked if I had a computer. I said "Yes". Then she asked "Is it in the house?". I said "Yes".
She then asked if she could see it and seemed quite distraught. So I invited her in because she was very hesitant to come in when I had first opened the door.

Well, in she came and looked for my computer which I had in another room. Then she sat down and started to cry. This was quite a surprise as I had no idea if she was ill or O.K. So I offered to make a cup of tea and asked her what this was all about?

The outcome of all this was that she had a dream during the night to come to my house to invite Jesus into her life. Apparently she had no intention of doing this. The dream had continued as she needed confirmation that this was the right thing to do. - So in the dream The Lord had said to ask me if I had a computer in the house.

Well she was not sure which house I lived in but knew the name of the street. At the party we had exchanged our home addresses just in case we would like to meet up during the year.

Also I had told her at the Christmas Party that I was a Christian and that I would pray for her when she asked me to, for whatever it was at the time. I said to her if she became a Christian she could pray herself.

Well that part did not go down very well because she said there was no sense in inviting Jesus into her life but if I wanted to pray she would be happy for me to do that.

Back to my lounge room:

I brought in a cup of tea for us and asked her to explain why she had come. She said she was not sure apart from the fact that she had never had such a dream before and that she wanted to check out whether or not I had a computer in the house. Also she needed to know if God was real or was it all a figment of her imagination?

Knowing now that I did have a computer she said she would go.

I said to her that I would like to ask before she left what she knew about being Born Again and becoming a Christian? She could not understand that when you invite Jesus into your life you are Born again into the Kingdom of God.
    She wanted proof of this so I showed her in my Bible:
      Starting at - John Chapter 3 verse 3.
  (It says: Jesus replied, "Very truly I tell you, no one can see
    the Kingdom of God without being born again.")

You can look this up if you are not sure what I am talking about. It would be better than me trying to explain what Jesus said.

After much talking and discussion she thought that yes, maybe it was God talking to her during the night, so was prepared to make a commitment to invite Jesus in because she needed help in her life at that time.

The outcome of all this is that I was able to lead her in Prayer and Praise The Lord she did it!

Then doubt suddenly came to her and she said she would like to talk to our Minister (Priest) at the Church to know that I was qualified to do this .

I did tell her that I always needed to report to my Minister and let him know what had taken place. It was a really good thing that she wanted to tell him herself.

Yes it was all of God.

For many years God used that lady very much in our Church, especially utilizing the lovely gifts and talents that He had given her for His Praise and Glory.

Also she helped to distribute Bibles for Evangelism to another Country.
          Amen.

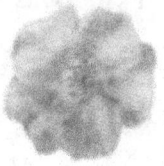

Note:

Our God is an awesome God, even using our Dream time to talk to us and guide us.
However we do need to be obedient to listen and act on what He tells us to do.

What a lovely blessing it was that this lady, listened and acted on what she had dreamt about.

After this encounter she had a lovely life on this earth with Jesus in her life every day.

.....

> *James: 5 verse 16*
>
> *The Effectual Fervent Prayer*
> *of a*
> *Righteous Man*
> *Availeth Much.*

A Young Woman

A good few years ago I used to run a morning group for young Mums and their children at our Local Church. This was quite successful for about eight years. I used to go early to unlock the door of the building that was used for our Church hall, to set up and get ready for the morning meeting. So it was a surprise to see a young woman (whom I had never met) sitting on the step by the doorway.
I said "Hello, we haven't met before, have you come to see me?" Whereupon she burst into tears and said she didn't know what to do. A friend had apparently been telling her about the group. Because it was held at the Church, she thought it would be best to come as she had no-one to help with some problems. She had plucked up courage to come that morning.

As we sat talking I said really you need Jesus in your life. He is the only one that can really help you, is that why you have come? She said she had thought about that but didn't know how to do it.

Sitting outside I was able to lead her in the prayer to invite The Lord Jesus into her heart. After that she calmed down so we went inside where I put the kettle on to make her a cup of tea. We continued to talk, having a good counselling session before other members of the group arrived.

The outcome of this is that she became a regular member of the group bringing her small child and a baby each time, making new friends and coming to Church. Praise The Lord! She was surprised that when she asked me to Pray for her and her family that The Lord answered her prayers as well. One time I prayed for healing of her small daughter who I visited in Hospital. Then later that day she was able to take her home perfectly well.   Amen.

Our God is a God of Surprises!

What does our God say about a Woman?

*****

You can read this in Proverbs
Chapter 31 verses 10 - 31.

*****

This is what it says in verse 30:
Charm is deceptive
And beauty is fleeting;
But a woman who
Fears the LORD
Is to be praised.

*****

We know that we are not to be frightened of
The LORD.
Just to be happy to do His will
And keep
His commandments.
Then to live a good life here on this earth.

Newspaper Bible Quote:

I have a Studio on the back of our house for my Paintings and Art Work. One afternoon a week I hold Painting lessons on our back Patio - mostly for ladies. One of the students came and set up as usual, being a bit early for her lesson (just her and myself were there at the time).

Having put her easel up and starting to paint on her latest oil painting, I went to check on her progress. She asked if she could talk about something other than the painting - I said "Yes of course you can, what is it?"

Well each week in our local newspaper at the time, there was a Christian Text - a small Scripture reading and each week she had been reading them. Knowing that I was a Christian she asked if I knew who put them in because they were in as anonymous.

I said if it says anonymous no one knows who it is.

My student then asked if I could answer some questions about God and what did it mean when it said you have to be Born Again.

As I started to explain, I realized that God had sent her when the tears started falling down her cheeks. She did not understand, because she said she was not crying and was most embarrassed that the tears were happening while we were talking.

I said 'Praise The Lord' because - knowing that I was a Christian she was happy to talk and learn but did not realize that it was The Holy Spirit of Jesus touching her heart to invite Jesus into her life.

To cut a long story short, I can say - as she sat there while we talked, she did just that when I lead her in prayer to invite Jesus into her life.

Afterwards her face glowed at the revelation that she understood.

<blockquote>
I gave her a big Christian Hug and welcomed her into
The Kingdom of our God.
Praise the Lord.
</blockquote>

I still did not let her know that it was myself who had been putting the Scriptures in the Newspaper each week for a few years. - It however was confirmation to me that God used them for His Glory.

So that was very good.
Amen.

Another Student:

I used to give holiday 'Oil Painting Lessons' because ours is a tourist Town with people coming to stay sometimes up to three months to get away from the colder Winter in the South.

One lady who came, (The Lord brought her I am sure) I invited to come to Church if she would like to. However she said no thank you as she was camping in a tent and could say her prayers there.
Well I was pleased that she prayed, so assumed she was a Christian.

The next week she asked me what it meant when it said you need to be Born Again? I explained to her but she was not in agreement with me. So I gave her a leaflet regarding the Sinners Prayer and asked if she would like to read it sometime in her tent because I knew that she liked reading during the evenings.

Anyway she took it because she had told me she had never asked Jesus into her life thinking it was not necessary.

Well the following week she came (it was the last painting lesson for her as she had come to the end of her holiday), she gave me the biggest hug and said she had done it!

I thought she meant she had finished her painting - she used to sit and paint in the tent.

No - she said - not about the painting, she had invited Jesus into her life sitting on the floor of her tent and she said the tent seemed to be filled with the presence of The Lord.

She was so happy and travelling around on her own she knew she would never be lonely again that Jesus would always be with her.

Praise The Lord.   *Amen.*

Russian Lady

We all looked forward to meeting the wife of one of our congregation members, who had recently (at that time) gone to another country to marry his new bride.

He had been a bachelor and we never envisaged him being married as he was a very quiet young man. Then in his late thirties he went to Russia for a holiday and fell in love with a young woman there. After that he made quite a few trips to get to know her and her family over a couple of years.

With great anticipation we awaited the day that he would bring his new bride to Church, expecting her to be a very homely looking person because of the way he was.

Well what a surprise - she was the most beautiful young woman, so lovely and they were obviously very much in love.

There was just one thing missing in the relationship and that being - she was not a Christian. Her new husband had tried to explain to her the importance of having Jesus in her life but with the difference in languages it was hard for her to understand that he thought it was necessary.

So after Church a good few months later while we were having morning tea, I believed God wanted me to talk about this to her. I asked if she would come over and sit in a quiet corner with me.

The Holy Spirit guided me to talk about the Prayer to lead her to invite Jesus into her life.

Then Praise The Lord she wanted to do it - So we did.

Her husband was over joyed when we told him and also our Minister what had just taken place.

No other God has authority to do this only Jesus Christ our Lord who allows His Holy Spirit to Minister through us as Christians.

Yes we are to evangelize and to encourage lost souls to come into the Kingdom of God.

Praise The Lord!

They had a wonderful happy marriage and produced two lovely children.

Just think, God can use us if we are willing,
whenever He needs us.

Amen

Jesus is Lord

Removal Man

We had to move from our property near the City of Perth in Western Australia and travel 1,000 kilometers North to a rental property on a Plantation. This would be our new home for the next two and half years while we decided what best to do next.

That sets the scene for our move North. Not having enough money for the normal removal people, we hired a friend with a truck who had a friend with another truck. Well the friend of the friend was not a suitable person really to do this as he had no patience to carefully load our treasured possessions.

We could not very easily back out of this deal, so it was a great drama with the back of the vehicle not having doors that closed properly. Therefore everything got covered in dust that blew in through the gaps in the doors, while driving the 1,000 kilometres North.

Arriving at our so called new home, things were almost falling out of the back of the truck (that was the friend of the friend's truck). I was very cross with the owner driver. He seemed so angry after the long twelve hour drive and was just swearing as he pulled our furniture out of the back of his vehicle, blaspheming God, also the name of Jesus as he did so.

I stood up to him and said that I am a Christian and I pray that Jesus will get hold of you one day and turn your life upside down and the right side up!

I would not like to print his reply to that!!

We stayed on that property for those two and a half years before purchasing and living in our next home. Then about a year after while living in this house the removal man found us and knocked on the door. After all those years we had forgotten the drama hoping not to see him again.

But no - there he was on the front door step saying 'Hello' and could he come in? I said "No you can't", my husband heard him and said to me "Get rid of him he is not coming in here".

Anyway I went outside telling him I was sorry but my husband did not want to talk to him. Not to be outdone he said "Mrs. I am a Christian now and it's all your fault"

I said "I don't believe you as you told us so may lies before".

He had a bag in his hand offering it to me with Videos in. So I told him I was not interested in what I thought would be offensive ones.

Then he told me they were Christian ones by an Evangelist and that he really was a Christian and please would I listen to what he wanted to tell me.

We were still outside the house talking. Apparently he had been in hospital very ill with cancer - while in there he remembered what I had said about Jesus. So he prayed that if Jesus was real He would heal him - so Jesus did - and this man had his life turned upside down and right side up.

He had been trying to find me to say thank you.

There is a bit more to the story. He had brought his new wife that he believed The Lord had found for him, whom he had left along the road in their motel room. So asked - could he bring her to meet me?

It was hard for my husband to believe any of this but he agreed that yes he could bring her a bit later that day.

This is really a good God Story. Amen.

The couple then went on to spread the Gospel,
hopefully converting people to become Christians.

Jesus is Lord

The Vine!

John Chapter:
15 verses 5 - 9

Jesus says "I am the vine, you are the branches. If you remain in me and I in you, you will bear much fruit, apart from me you can do nothing. If you do not remain in me, you are like a branch that is thrown away and withers, such branches are picked up, thrown into the fire and burned. If you remain in me and my words remain in you, ask whatever you wish and it will be done for you. This is to my Father's glory, that you bear much fruit, showing yourselves to be my disciples. As the Father has loved me, so I have loved you.

Now remain in my love".

Jesus is Lord

Re: Bible Study

At one time each week we had a Bible Study. After a while it was just one person coming.

The last one staying to finish the course was a lady. She just loved the lessons and one day did admit that although going to Church most of her life she had never actually invited Jesus to be Lord of her life.

We talked about this, then I as able to lead her in prayer to become a Christian.

She had been embarrassed to admit that she had never done this, not thinking it was necessary as she was a good person, so she thought. Well after discussing about being good person, going to Church and looking after her family, I was able to say that going to Church does not make you a Christian.

It would be like going to McDonalds or Hungry Jacks each week would not turn you into a Hamburger!

That seemed a good illustration - so that's how come during our Bible Study Day she became Born Again as a Christian into God's Kingdom here on earth.

She looked so peaceful and happy after taking this step. This lady was able to cope with her everyday living better now that she had the Holy Spirit of Jesus, who would always be with her day by day to comfort and guide her wherever she would be.

After inviting Jesus to be Lord of her life, she was surprised that she had more confidence than she was used to.

Praise The Lord

Amen.

If you have never done a Bible Study -
Today maybe a good day to begin.
You can join a Bible Study group
or Study with a friend
or even on your own.
It can be very interesting.
*
During a Bible Study you will read True Stories relating to
God our Heavenly Father.

Skippy:

Along the boundary fence of our Orchard that we lived on at one time, was a hedge comprising of different types of grapes. They had not been looked after for a few years - just left to grow, pick, eat or sell. The bunches were the biggest we had ever seen, just beautiful reaching to the ground, too heavy almost to carry one bunch. One of our Greyhound dogs named 'Skippy', a really large light brown colour brindle, used to walk over the Lady Finger grapes and with his mouth just pick off one grape, lay down and enjoy eating it, then go sometimes for another one.
It was so special to watch this great big dog being so dainty.

No this is not really a God Story - but it is a true Story.

God Loves our Pets as well as He Loves Us.

Just thought I would put this in with the drawing of the grapes.

✝

As Christians The Lord will renew our strength.
This is a true Story from The Bible - you will find this verse
in the book of Isaiah.

Isaiah Chapter 40 verse 31.

But those who hope in The LORD they will renew their strength.
They will soar on wings like eagles, they will run and not grow weary, they will walk and not be faint.

Prayer

Dear God I pray that I may be filled with
Righteousness that comes through your
Son Jesus Christ (Philippians: 1 v 11)
I pray that Jesus may be Lord of my life
for ever and ever.

May I grow in your love God and be
filled evermore with your Holy spirit,
also with your fruits and gifts of the Holy Spirit.
That you may use me to help others.
I pray that I may be so filled with your love,
peace and joy that it may emanate through me
for others to see.

That they may come to know Jesus,
That He died for us on the cross.
I pray that my sins are forgiven,
- please God and help me to know when
You have forgiven me each time - Please God,
so that I can feel that release in my Spirit
to do your will each day and for ever.

I pray that I never forget or take for granted
that Jesus died for my sins on the cross,
that only through Him am I saved.
Giving you my body for your Holy Spirit
to work through and use as a temple for you God.
May I ever know your saving grace
and live in your Kingdom forever.
Amen.

Let us pray for our Country

This is our Country, this is our land, dear God it is beautiful, most parts too beautiful to describe.

We have wonderful landscapes, oceans, a vast expanse of sky. Most beautiful creatures you have given us in our Country to love and cherish, to look at and appreciate.

Giant Whales in the ocean, tiny sea creatures and all the land animals, wild and tame.

This is our Country and I praise you Heavenly Father that you allow us to live, work and play here.

Help us to look after this country in the right way.

I pray that you will bless this land with sun and rain for producing the crops to feed the population of people here, also all the abundance of animals and sea creatures in this Country and throughout the world.

May your peace reign with us here, may many come into Salvation today dear God throughout this land.

                         Amen.

Jesus is Lord

The Author Jessie Larman was born in England. She married in 1958, emigrated to Australia in 1973 with her Husband Patrick Larman and their three young children.

A Naturalized Australian Citizen, Jessie is fortunate to have Grandchildren and Great Grandchildren

She was healed of an incurable disease in 1984 in Perth, Western Australia. Jessie at the moment is living in Carnarvon, North West Australia. Here she has her Art Studio and is actively involved with her Anglican Church, World Wide Mothers Union, Desktop Publishing, Oil Painting etc...

She is widely known and loved by many Carnarvon residents. Jessie is a wonderful witness of the Love of our Lord God to all those that are privileged to know her.

...

In Prayer Let Your Soul Soar
as on the wings of
an Eagle.

Index - List of Stories

Stories	Page No.
My Journey	8
Light of God	12
Lunch Time Deliverance	14
The Lord Worked Quickly	15
What's in a Name	16
Cruise Ship Story	18
Healing of Back	24
Story of Pat	28
Healing as he went	34
The Computer	36
A Young Woman	40
Newspaper Bible Quote:	42
Another Student	44
Russian Lady	46
Removal Man	48
Re: Bible Study	52
Skippy	54

Extra's

The Lords Prayer	17
To be a Christian	27
Love is the Greatest Thing	32
23rd. Psalm	35
To be a Woman	41

Extra's Cont'd....	Page
The Vine	51
Prayer	56
Pray for our Country	57

Harry Cat.

Thank You Lord that you Bless
Our
Families
&
Pets.

Praise God

As Christians our names are written in the Lamb's Book of Life.

Revelation Chapter: 21 verse 27.

Jesus is Lord

I.S.B.N. Number 978-0-9872075-0-0

Romans: 1 verse 16

For I am not ashamed

of the

Gospel of Christ

www.ingramcontent.com/pod-product-compliance
Lightning Source LLC
Chambersburg PA
CBHW080126020526
44112CB00036B/2731